The New Google SEO (Search Engine Optimization)

What You Need to be Successful in The New Google SEO

Kathleen McDivitt

ANGELICO BOOKS

Table of Contents

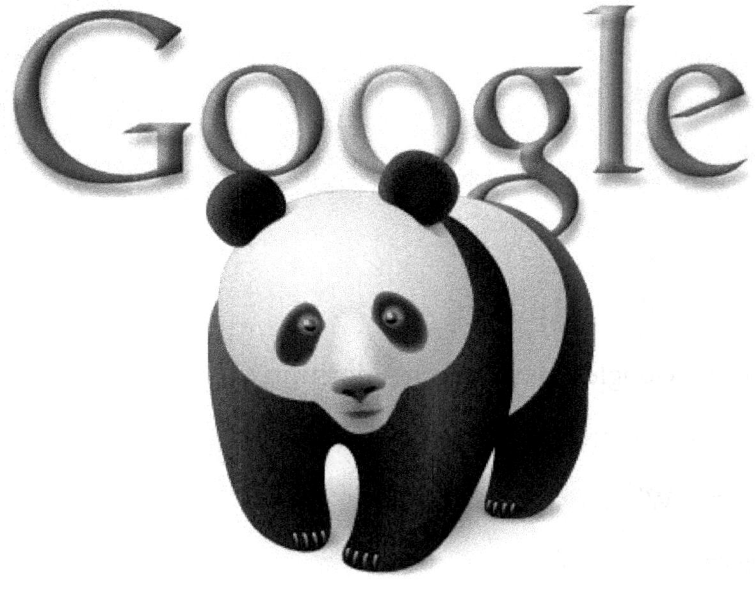
Google

Chapter 1—Google's New Search Algorithm

In February 2011, the world of search engine optimization changed fundamentally when Google unveiled a search engine filter named after a Google engineer, Mr. Navneet Panda.

The Google Panda filter has affected almost 12% of all search results. So, if your pages have suddenly disappeared from the search results and you are getting a lot less traffic, know that you are not alone.

This isn't just some small algorithmic change, like adding locks to car doors. This is a huge shift in the way search works—like the shift from horse and buggy to the car. It's a new mindset.

Old techniques are not going to work in the same way anymore. You are going to have to make changes and do things differently.

When you understand this and act on it, you will find that your traffic increases dramatically. But, if you do not act on it and make the necessary changes, you might as well start looking somewhere else for traffic, because if you have not been affected by Google Panda now, chances are you will be. And if you are not hit by Panda, you probably will be affected by Penguin. We will be delving into both of them despite their slightly different targets.

If you are picking up this book, you are probably already familiar with the drastic changes in Google Search that started in April 2011. Maybe you've read other books on Search Engine Optimization or talked to a lot of people who are "experts". Perhaps, you have a good, solid understanding of SEO, or you may be completely brand new and just picking this up and going, "You know, I have to do something about this." Regardless of your situation, this book will be of interest and value to you.

I'm guessing your goal is to rank highly on the keywords that bring you money, clients, or fulfill your dreams in some way, AND have some sense of certainty that once you do all that hard work to achieve those high rankings, you will keep them!

This book explains how the dramatic changes Google has recently made to its search algorithms will affect you and gives pointers on how to receive and maintain good, high quality traffic from Google after the changes.

I have been a professional SEO consultant working with private clients since 1999. I've worked on everything from selling clothing and furniture online, to helping government agencies use the Internet to improve health and stop smoking. I've seen it all. I have watched the rise and fall of link farms, I have talked to all the pundits, and I have read the books. I have had clients who were hit by Google Panda; and honestly, I had to scramble to figure out how to recover.

Most people, even those who are SEO specialists in Google, do not explain Google Panda in a way that the average person can understand. So this book is for both the average person, and for SEO experts who want to have all of the latest information collected in one place. I've found actually that most people, even most "SEO specialists," are still caught in the old paradigm.

Let's start with some common myths.

MYTH ONE: Good keyword research is finding keywords with the highest number of searches in my market. FALSE. Keyword research is still critical, and now it's all about doing **targeted** keyword research. In the old paradigm, people looked for the keywords that had the maximum number of hits. In this new paradigm, what you are looking for is the keywords that are most aligned with your content. This is a fairly dramatic change.

MYTH TWO: I gotta have tons of content. FALSE. While SEO is still about building good content, the focus is now on the quality of the content, and engaging the audience. It used to be that (in the very old days, when I got started) a website was basically an online brochure. You put it up and you left it there. Good content was considered 500 words that were spelled right and grammatically correct, and included our keywords. Now content must be fresh, meaningful and long. The new realilty is that lots of bad or short content can actually harm your search rankings.

MYTH THREE: I can buy lots of cheap links to build page rank. FALSE. Actually, Google Panda was initially targeted at link farms because people had all sorts of schemes established. I still get spam in my mailbox saying, "We'd like to do a three-way link with you! We'd like to trade links with you," because I have such a high page rank on my site. Getting links is still important, but quality counts.

Getting low quality links can actually hurt your site rankings. In fact, with Google Penguin an entire industry has sprung up that helps people get rid of incoming links that they actually paid money to get! That's how much of a turn-around there has been in the industry!

MYTH FOUR: Each page is an island. FALSE. In the old days (2011), each page was considered an island - so we optimized them individually separate from the rest of the site or site segment. Now, in the new paradigm, Google looks at sections of sites, or entire sites. So, if you have some really well done pages that are just doing everything right, but you also have pages that have broken links, junk content, or too many ads, then those junk pages could really be pulling down the whole rest of your site.

Understanding this new paradigm and how it impacts you is the core of this book. Google Panda is essentially a shift away from a mechanized process of search to an expert system focused on evaluating entire sites, their reputations, and the user experience.

I am going to start by going over Google's goals and then focus on Google Panda itself. It is critical to have a really clear understanding of where Google is coming from and to be able to think like Google. This will allow you to be able to understand the big picture and remain competitive.

The second piece I will cover is Google Panda. What are it's goals? What is the software attempting to do? Answering these questions will allow us to better understand how to can respond to the changes.

Our third step is to discuss how to know if you have been hit. For example, if suddenly your traffic has gone down it may be that you have been hit by Google Panda or perhaps it may be that there is something else going on.

Fourth, we'll talk about Google Penguin and how that might impact your website.

Finally I'll discuss step-by-step SEO in the post-Panda, post-Penguin world, what exactly you need to do, and how to put together a plan and track your success.

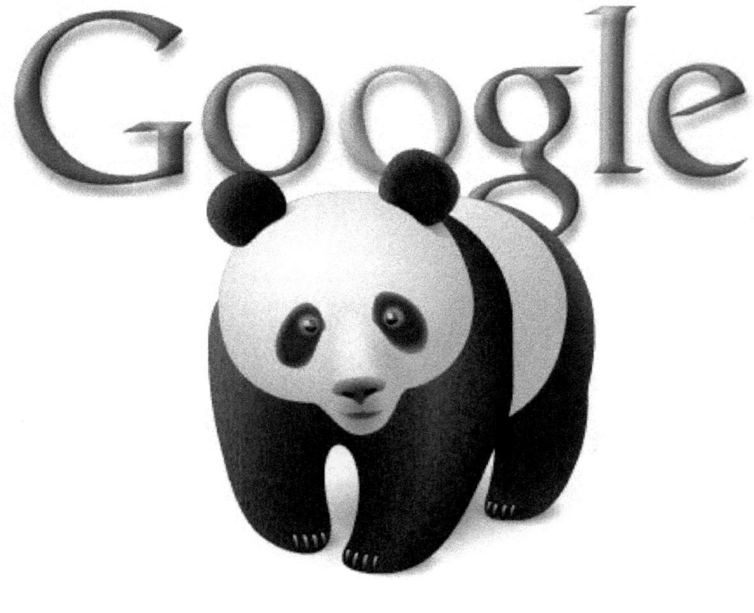
Google

Chapter Two—Understanding Google's Goals

I n the post-Panda world, Google has two very clear goals.

Provide the Right Answer Quickly

The first goal is to provide the fastest possible answer to the searcher's question, so the user continues to use Google and thus Google makes money. Research shows that when people are looking for something specific—say a book on relationships—they will do a search and click on a link (usually the coveted top link). They will then spend less than 1 second looking at the page before making two critical decisions:

1. Does this page have what I want?
2. Do I trust this content?

Google's goal is to make sure that the top results of the search for that keyword are most likely to have the user say "YES" to those two questions.

Increase Visitor Engagement

The second goal that Google wants is to provide sites that have the highest level of engagement. I will be talking about engagement a lot throughout the book. But basically these are sites that are highly trusted and provide value. Google wants to show the most relevant pages with the highest quality available on the web, so people immediately get what they want or need and continue to use Google as a search engine.

Traditionally, Google used on-site metrics like number of words on the page, keyword density (how many times the keyword or key phrase is used on the site), or quality incoming links to assess the quality. That has gotten less and less effective.

The Challenge: Rogue SEO Specialists

The challenge for Google is that there are thousands of new sites created daily, many of which are junk. Over time, search engine optimizers have learned how to game the system; to make bare minimum, low-quality writing so that it is just high enough in quality to pass the test and keep it above being detected as spam. This causes a lot of problems and complaints from users. Google wants to be able to avoid this and provide the very best results.

Why does Google want to do this? Google wants people to use them as a search engine, that's how Google makes its money. To remain competitive and be people's first choice as a search engine, Google needs to win peoples' trust by providing good content and editing out all the junk. So, how does Google decide what is good and what is bad? This is where Google Panda comes into play.

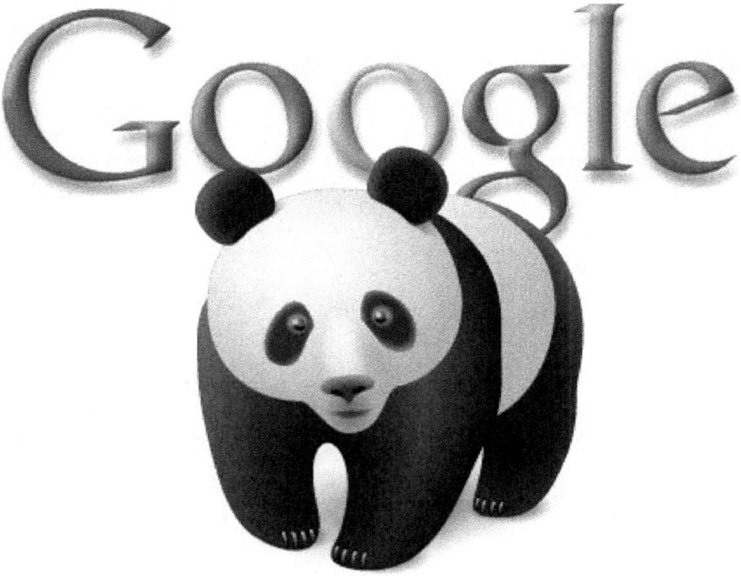
Google

Chapter Three—What is Google Panda?

Google Panda is a filter designed to weed out low quality pages. If a site has a large number of low quality pages, Google Panda will flag the entire site. Even if you have some great content but your site happens to contain some junk, your entire site could be flagged. This filter runs periodically every four to seven weeks. This is the reason why your site can be doing just fine and then suddenly disappear from the search engine rankings.

How was Google Panda designed? This story is quite interesting. Google, in trying to make their search engines as effective as possible, hired a bunch of outside human quality testers and asked them to go through and rate different sites using a list of specific questions.

They asked them to rate the sites based on three areas: on quality, design, and trustworthiness. And, trustworthiness was a big factor.

They asked questions like:

- Would you give this site your credit card?
- Would you buy medication for your children from this site?
- Do you think this site is easy to use?

With this information gathered, they created two groups of sites. They put all the sites that the human quality testers liked in one group and all the sites that they did not like into another group. Then they created a massive computer program to mimic the human raters. This is where the name Panda comes into play. Mr. Panda is the man who actually created the groundbreaking algorithm to speed the processing up so the program would not take 5 years to run.

I am going to use this analogy to demonstrate this process. I am shopping at the local mall, looking for a specific type of clogs, and you are sitting on a bench watching me. In this analogy, I am a user and you are Google. I go into a store and I come out immediately. You might guess one of two things: either a) I did not see what I wanted; or b) the store itself did not appeal to me in some way.

So, I go into another store and I stay there for a couple of minutes, but then I come out. (Now, keep in mind you are going to be able to see when I am holding a package or not, but Google in reality cannot necessarily see that. At least, I do not think they can!) I go into another store and come out in a couple of minutes and you are probably going to guess that store also did not offer shoes or at least not the clogs that I wanted.

Then, you might see me go into another store and I stay there for like 5 minutes. But in this example, that is still not long enough to really buy a pair of shoes. So, I come out and you think—maybe that store did have clogs and I tried them on but they did not have them in my size.

12

What I am trying to get at with this example is that Google Panda looks at what the user actually does on a site. This is a huge difference with Google Panda.

In the old days of search engine optimization, Google would look at backlinks, the length of the content on the page, and various mechanized statistics about the site itself to determine the quality of the site. Now, in the new paradigm, Google Panda looks at how people use the site.

Using my story as an example, it might be that in the old paradigm, Google would go and look in that store and see that it had shoes, or at least it had signs that said "Shoes" and signs that said "Clogs." They would look at how many other people went into that store to decide whether it actually was a good store for clogs. Now, it actually looks at people who say "I want clogs," and sees how long those people stay in the store. And of course, this is the same for other examples too.

When you look at it that way, it is a complete shift in how you need to look at your search engine optimization. Some of the sites that have been hit hardest include:

- **E-commerce with low quality product pages.** For example, a shoe store that has "Clogs" written all over it but there is no actual description of the clogs; just lots of junk content.
- **Affiliate sites with limited content.**These are sites that are selling other products or selling information products, but they have very few pages and the pages are not unique.
- **Sites that are hard to use, or only designed to make money through AdSense.** One of the challenges with these sites is

that they often have a lot of advertising that actually obscures the user's ability to access the information. This is something that I will discuss further later on.

Chapter Four—The Critical (and Potentially Devastating) Differences in the New Search Engine Optimization Paradigm

There are two major differences with this new paradigm. The first one is that the Panda update is all about user feedback signals. In other words, Google is carefully analyzing how people are interacting with your site and using this analysis to measure quality.

Understanding Your Bounce Rate

You want to start to think like a customer and increase the amount of time the right customers spend on your site. One of the things that Google uses to determine whether your site matches a particular keyword is "bounce rate."

Google's support (http://docs.google.com/support.google.com) defines bounce rate as "the percentage of single page visits or visits in which the person left your site from the entrance or landing page." If you receive a high bounce rate, your landing pages are viewed as not being relevant to your visitors.

When you design your landing pages to match your keywords and ads, your pages will be more engaging to your visitors and they will stay longer on your site and convert. It is extremely important for these pages to contain the information and/or service(s) that were promised in the ad copy or link from Google.

What does all this mean? I am going to use the clog example again to explain. We will use "Clog" as our keyword. You are a store that only sells clogs. You do not sell any other shoes.

You may, in the old search paradigm, want to optimize for the keyword "Shoes" because a lot more people are looking for shoes than they are looking for clogs. Doing that would provide you with a lot more traffic, so if you measured your success by how much traffic you are getting then optimizing for shoes might be a better option.

In the new world this could hurt your rankings. Say, I am looking for running shoes and your clog site comes up near the top of the list, so I click on it. Within a second, it is obvious that you do not sell running shoes, so I click back. This is considered a "bounce." So your site will actually get a negative search engine ranking because I clicked "back" so quickly. I clicked on the site and then I clicked back to Google, in doing so, indicating to them that this site is not a good match for the word "shoes."

Now, if you were using some of the techniques that we are going to be talking about later, you might just optimize for the word "clogs" in which case, I might search "clogs" and come to your site. Then, I might spend a few more minutes on your site deciding if it has what I want, and if I trust the site enough to give it my credit card. If I spend over 2 minutes on the site—even if I don't buy anything—it shows Google that the site may actually be about clogs, and that it's a good match.

In the new SEO paradigm, Google is determining search ranking on different metrics. They are looking at bounce rate (as discussed earlier), so if a searcher does not have a good first impression of your site or does not think your site has what they want, they are going to click on to another listing. Even if your site has the most useful and compelling content in the world, but the searcher doesn't know that because you have bad design or too many ads, you'll get penalized when the visitor searcher leaves the site.

Click Through Rate

Google also looks at the "Click Through Rate," which is when the searcher clicks onto additional pages from the page where the search word took them. So I might come to your clog site and on the home page you have many images of clogs. If I "click through" to another page by clicking on one of those images and going to a page specifi-cally for that clog, then your "click through rate" has increased. This again is a measure of people being interested in your content.

Other things that Google considers include:

- the number of pages viewed by the searcher
- whether the searcher returns to the site
- whether they mention your company in social media

- if your pages are printed out by searchers
- if searchers are using the scroll bar, which indicates that they are actually reading the content

Taking all of this into consideration, it is crucial for your site to not only attract the right people, but to also get them to stay longer and take more action within your site. And in the next chapter, I will outline what exactly you need to be thinking about in order to make that happen.

Chapter Five—Introducing Google Penguin

On May 25, 2012 Google released a new update to their algorithm (search engine program) called Google Penguin. The purpose of Google Penguin is to penalize sites that:

- use low quality content (web spam)
- use maniplulative linking practices
- over-optimize their sites

What do these really mean?

Low Quality Content

We've been talking a lot about content. Let's get down and dirty about what you can no longer get away with in the Google Search-verse.

1. **Poorly written content.** Having poorly written, meaningless articles written for you and putting them up in article engines or on your blog. While some article engines still can provide you with good backlinks, the articles themselves must be well-written, interesting, and add value to the viewer. This means no spun content (if you don't know what spun content is—great!).

2. **Old content.** Google is placing more and more emphasis on "freshness." This means that the old brochure style sites, where you put content up and forget about it, is no longer going to work. Sites that have regular new information will get more page rank and thus more traffic.

3. **Used content.** The content you have on your site must be unique. If it's posted somewhere else on the web, it's considered duplicate content and will not help you.

4. **Keyword density.** From Wikipedia: "Keyword density is the percentage of times a keyword or phrase appears on a web page compared to the total number of words on the page. In the context of search engine optimization keyword density can be used as a factor in determining whether a web page is relevant to a specified keyword or keyword phrase." This means that your keywords should be in your text a "natural" percentage of times. What we're looking at post-Panda is 5-8% keyword density as optimal. This gives Google (and your readers) enough keywords to know what the site is about, but not so many that it looks unnatural.

5. **Content (or sites) with links that go nowhere.** Google rewards sites that are well maintained. So clean up those broken links or links to sites that no longer exist! One tool you can use

to explore your links is **www.majesticseo.com**. (*Disclaimer*: Site live as of publishing this book. We have no relationship with this vendor.)

Manipulative Linking

Since the dawn of the Internet, search engines have used incoming links as a tool to evaluate how valuable people think your content is. If lots of people are putting links to your site on their sites, then whatever is on your site must be valuable, which is why they show it to their customers.

This breaks down when SEO consultants start to manipulate the system by getting lots of links from questionable sources. Penalizing manipulative linking is the heart of Penguin. This one change is really shaking up the industry because the mainstay of most SEO firms is getting links for clients. With the new updates those links can actually harm the ranking of the site. This should serve as a warning: if a company offers (for a small fee) to get you lots of backlinks, ask informed questions.

Here are the things to avoid in links:

1. **Lots of links from the same company or group of companies.** If Google sees that you have a lot of links from one site, or a bunch of sites all in the same network, it looks questionable. This could be a link farm and this is exactly the type of activity that Penguin is designed to penalize. Not only does it not do you any good, it can actually harm your ranking. That's why people are paying to get unlinked.

2. **Links from sites that are not relevant.** If you have a clog shop and you are getting most of your links from sites that are in completely different markets or parts of the world, it looks suspicious, especially if combined with the other activities.

3. **Links that are on pages that have a bunch of dissimilar links.** The classic link-scheme is that you pay someone to give you links and they go off and pay other people to put your links on their sites. But these sites have multiple links, usually all in a group, for completely different products and services. These look like exactly what they are—purchased links. Google does not support purchased links.

4. **Links from low-quality blogs.** One way people get around these linking schemes is to create blogs that have real content on them and put links in the blogs. Unfortunately (for SEO folks) and fortunately (for consumers) Google is getting better and better at identifying these blogs as being created expressly for SEO, and penalizing links from them.

5. **Link trading.** I regulary get emails from people asking me to trade links with them. I'll put a link on your site if you put one on mine. This is discouraged, although if it's relevant it can be okay. It depends on the anchor text used.

The other aspect of links that Google Penguin looks at is anchor text. What is anchor text? This is the text that you actually click on to get to the linked page. If you look at the image on the next page, the anchor text is the text in blue "Webmaster Central Blog."

Update *April 11:* We've rolled out this algorithmic change globally to all English-language Google users and incorporated new signals as we iterate and improve. We'll continue testing and refining the change before expanding to additional languages. You can learn more on our <u>Webmaster Central Blog</u>.

Posted by Amit Singhal, Google Fellow, and Matt Cutts, Principal Engineer

Our goal is that our anchor text looks natural—that it looks like the text that someone might use who is not an SEO expert.

If you sell clogs, you might want your anchor text to always say "clogs" or "buy clogs" or "brandname clogs", but in the real world, most people who write about your clogs might actually put something more like: if you want some great clogs Click Here, and the link would be Click Here. Or they might say: visit karens-kooky-clogs.com and that would be the link.

So what do we need to do? That's right, make our anchor text look "more natural."

Here are the metrics we've gleaned. Have anchor text variation with an ideal mix:

- 60% of your anchors generic (click here or the URL of your site)
- 30% phrase based, so the following might be the whole link "click here for information on the amazing red clogs I bought last week"
- 10% an exact match: "clogs" or "brandname clogs"

There are two ways to change your link profile and your anchor profile: add new high-quality links, and remove low-quality links. The first step though is to understand your current link profile. We're going to suggest some tools for this later in the book.

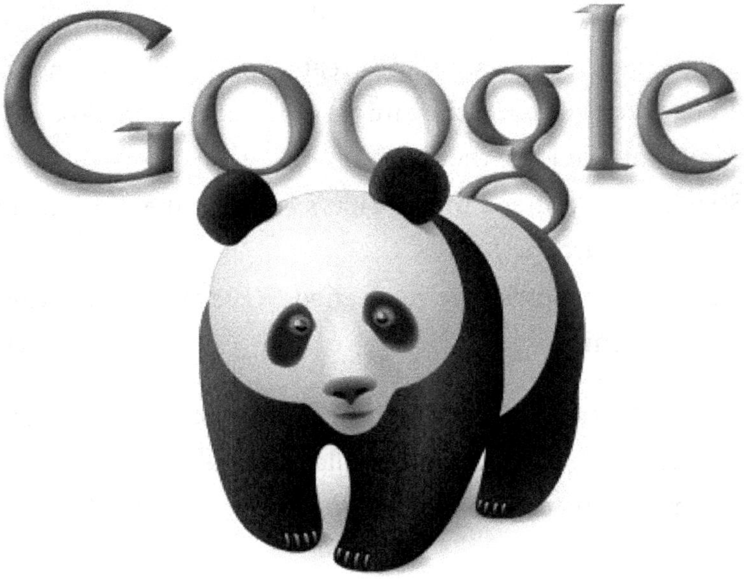
Google

Chapter Six—Creating a SEO Plan that Works for Now (and in the Future)

There are five important things that you can do to make people want to come to your site, stay longer, and take more action. The first one is doing keyword research and using keywords that really target your content and target your market. The second one is to increase your page "stickiness." The third one is to create and design a user experience that builds trust. The fourth one is to generate user-generated content, or to have user-generated content. Fifth is to really build your brand.

SEO Plan 1: Keyword Research

You want to make sure your keywords are very closely targeted to what you do. Remember, if a visitor comes to your site then clicks back to Google, it's not just a lost visitor, but it can actually negatively impact your rankings!

For example, let's say we own a leadership training company. We could decide to optimize the site for the word "leadership." It looks like a great word—a lot of people searching for leadership. You might think, so many people are searching for leadership, we will optimize the site for leadership and get all that wonderful traffic!

That might have worked for you in the old world, if you had a big budget for optimization. But, the challenge is that most people searching for "leadership" are not looking for leadership training.

The keyword "leadership" is too broad. People looking for a definition of leadership, or leadership quotes, or leadership books might land on your site, see that you don't offer any of those things, stay less than a second and click the Back button. Prior to Panda, that was neutral—it did not help you, and it did not hurt you. In the new paradigm, it hurts you. It means somebody has come to your store using the keyword 'leadership' and left. It means that Google will then discount you as somebody that has anything to do with leadership which is exactly what you do not want.

Choosing the Right Keywords

Google offers a free keyword research tool. I highly recommend using this to source your keywords. Go to Google.com, type "Google free research tool," and then type in your keywords. It will provide you with a listing of terms that people are typing into Google. The key is to think like a customer or potential customer: "OK, what would I type in if I were looking for me?" This will help you find the right keywords to match what you offer.

Another tip is to type in your competitors' URLs and see what keywords Google is ranking for them. Again, you can do this with the free Google keyword tool.

To do this for our example, "leadership training:"

1. Go to Google and type in your phrase: leadership training.
2. Write down the URLs of the top 5 companies that come up.
3. Go back to the Free Keyword Tool and put them into the website box
4. Review the keywords that come up and see which ones seem like a good fit for you.

You might find that some of those keywords are keywords that you want to use. You might also find that some of those keywords have nothing to do with what you offer at all, but the point here is that if you offer leadership training, you want to use the keywords that people are going to type in only if they are looking for what you offer.

Here is another example to further demonstrate. You are a portrait photographer. You do not want to optimize your site for the word "photographer" or "photography," as that would be too broad. There are going to be far to many people clicking onto and then immediately clicking off your site. You want to avoid that. So, what you want to do is to optimize for "portrait photographer" or "portrait photography" or the things that are in that specific area. And if you are a local portrait photographer in Boston, you want to focus your keywords on "portrait photographer Boston," so that you attract the right people and they stay. If you would like to learn more about local search engine optimization, we have another book that we wrote: *Local SEO: How To Get More Customers From Google, YELP & Yahoo* (www.amazon.com/dp/B006VHRBLM/)

SEO Plan 2: Increasing Visitor "Stickiness"

The first thing you want as a business owner is to have people coming to our site who are interested in what we offer. We want to use the right keywords.

Next, we want to make sure they find things that they want to read or view on our site. We want to make sure that we are "sticky."

Basically this means that we need unique and interesting content—blog posts, videos, audios, sales text, reviews, and white papers—anything that will get the visitor to come to your site stay awhile, and maybe even come back!

What we've been discussing is that the length of time somebody stays on your site makes a difference in your search engine rankings. We've found that if visitors stayed on a specific site for less than two minutes, and then clicked back (a bounce), they were given the opportunity to block the site if they were in Google Chrome.

That's kind of scary! Just think: if your site is blocked for a certain keyword then that is really going to give Google a clear indication that that keyword and your site are not a good fit. Our research showed that if the stay was more than seven minutes, then you are given the choice to Google Plus 1 that content, which means that you can show your friends that this site is really awesome. Essentially what this research indicates is that Google is looking for and rating page "stickiness."

What makes a page sticky? Or in other words, how does it attract and engage? Successful pages contain unique, well-written, relevant, and original content that is very highly attuned to the keyword(s). Containing over 750 words and high-quality images or video is optimal. Google has actually created a list of questions on Google Webmaster Central, which can be found at: http://googlewebmastercentral.blogspot.com/2011/05/more-guidance-on-building-high-quality.html

These are questions that you as a business owner or a webmaster should answer. These are the things you should ask yourself about your site to decide whether you are really building high quality content.

You are not going to be able to engage somebody for the required two minutes if you only provide 200 words of text and no links to additional information to get them to click further into your site. The more enticing and enriching the experience you can make for the searcher, the longer you are going to be able to hold their attention and have their visit counted as a positive mark for you. In achieving this, you set yourself above your competitors and establish a unique selling proposition.

SEO Plan 3: Building Trust in Your Website

The third element is creating a design that builds trust. One of the questions that were asked of the site testers on which the Google Panda algorithm is based was "Do you trust this site?"

Trust is a very emotional thing often times established in the first second that somebody sees your site before they have had a chance to read anything. That trust is built based on the look and feel of your design. Your goal is to create a design that is built for user engagement. It should be clean, simple, credible, and of high quality.

The questions you should ask yourself are:

- Is it well organized?
- Can the user easily find their way to the content that they want using clear navigation?
- Does the site load quickly? Site speed, which is how quickly the site loads, has been shown to directly affect bounce rates. We'll get into how to test site load speed later.
- What is the ad ratio? A high ad ratio negatively affects your trust, especially if those ads are near the top of your page.
- Are there too many ads?
- Do they get in the way of the visitor finding what they are looking for?
- There are also basic site hygiene issues to address:
- Does your site have broken links?
- Is there bad content?
- Is it outdated?

Some people have parts of their site that are just extremely well done with great content, then they have other parts of their site that are very old and look like they have been forgotten about. You used to be able to get away with this back in the days when each page was an island. However, now because a site is seen as a whole, those bad pages can really affect your rankings.

Canonical Tags

Another critical item is the failure to use canonical tags. This is whether the site URL has a "www." in front of it or not. SEO gurus go back and forth about whether this is important or not. I figure it's best to cover my bets and clean up canonical tags. Here's an example to explain why.

Let's say you have a company called Leadership Training Institute, and for some of your website's pages you use 'www.leadershiptraininginstitute.com', and on other pages it is just 'leadershiptraininginstitute.com'. Google will sometimes go through both of those sites looking at them as different sites. Now, suddenly you have two sets of the same content. It makes Google think that you have duplicate content which is, again, a negative mark on you. Correcting your URLs to be uniform is fairly easy based on the tools you are using—your webmaster should be able to make them uniform for you in less than an hour.

It is extremely important to go through the entire site with a fine tooth comb and remove broken links and bad content - making sure everything flows and there is continuity.

The Cost of Web Design

Here is a little insight I have gleamed from having owned a successful web design company for over ten years. There are three kinds of web design: bad web design, average web design, and great web design. Bad web design and great web design are both expensive. Average web design is not. You can get a design that is clean, simple, credible and of high quality for less than $500. I really recommend going to WordPress and finding somebody who is an expert in the platform to help you find a theme. The only drawback with an average website is that you basically need to accept it as it is—no changes.

Getting a custom website is like going to a tailor, giving them some ideas of what you want and requesting to have clothes made. My experience is that I always get what I ask for; but unless I'm really clear about what looks good on me, I rarely get something that looks fabulous. Most business people aren't designers; and honestly, most designers are not very good. On top of that, the business people (who don't know much about design) want to have input. Frankly, it's often a recipe for disaster.

A basic WordPress template is like going into a store and buying off the rack. In buying off the rack, you cannot ask the salesperson to change the sleeves of the shirt to a different color. You get what is available. It may be attractive, it may be quality material, it may fit beautifully, but it's not custom.

Unfortunately, often when a client is working with a pre-built template, (which is the cheapest kind of site to work with) they are going to go to their designer or whoever is putting up their site for them and say, "I really like this design but can you make all the links orange?" Doing this is going to increase your costs and also change a site that was designed to be well coordinated and attractive, to a site that may be hideous and unprofessional. So, please avoid doing this. It is best to buy a template off the shelf and accept it as it is.

On Page SEO

Now I would like to review the basics of on-page SEO. Again, there are other books on this, so I am not going to go into great detail. Aside from the things about creating a design that builds trust that I mentioned before, here are an additional five things that you want to make sure of with your website.

Title Tags

The title tag has two purposes. First it tells Google what your page is about. It's one of the top tools Google uses to understand what you want people to know about the site. Second, the title tag is often what people see in the search results that cause them to click on your site (see image below).

Most websites don't show it on the page itself. If you are using a tool like Wordpress, title tags are pretty easy to put in yourself. For other web design tools you may need more technology background to manipulate title tags.

Here are some guidelines when creating title tags:

- You want to have a title tag on every page.
- It should be under 60 characters.
- Your keywords should be located near the front of your tag.
- Remember we are using multi-word or long-tailed keywords. So, we are not using "leadership," we are using "leadership training for non-profits in Houston."

Meta Descriptions

Your meta description tag should be about 150 characters. Research shows you do not want it to be more than 150 characters, just like you do not want your title to be more that 60 characters. The meta description should contain a compelling reason why somebody should click on your listing. This does not have a lot of search engine weight, but instead a lot of customer weight, as it shows up in your search results under your title tag.

Here are some examples to help you understand this critical concept:

In the above image the title tag is: "SEO: The Free Beginner's Guide From SEOmoz." Notice that it is very targeted, full of keywords, and engaging.

The META tag is: "New to SEO? The Free Beginner's Guide to SEO has been read over 1 million times and provides the information you need to rank better." This is a great sales pitch for the book.

Compare this to:

I'm guessing that the SEO team for EthanAllen.com doesn't yet understand how title tags and meta tags show up in Google search results.

H1 Tags

The H1 header tag is going to be a headline on your page and you do want this to contain your keywords. So, if the home page for your leadership training site might have the title Leadership Training for Non-profits. This has two benefits:

1. It clearly states for your visitor what your site is about.
2. It reinforces to Google that your site is about leadership training.

You might have some variation in your keywords. So in your header tag, you might have "non-profit leadership training" and in the H1 tag, you have "non-profits." Having slightly different variations in wording makes it look like you are not spamming the system, and it also creates an opportunity for more people to find that page using different keywords. This is especially important given the changes introduced by Penguin.

Keyword Density

You want to use your keywords only three or four times. You do not want to overdo this, because then it looks like you are "keyword stuffing" and you can be penalized for that. The wording must look natural. Putting the keywords in bold or in bullets is a viable option to help show their importance.

The latest guidelines are that your keywords should be in your site at about 5%. So if your keyword is leadership training, and your page has 1000 words on it, 5% of them should be the phrase "leadership training." One of the things we've noticed with the latest Google Panda updates is it puts more emphasis on "over-optimizing" sites in both keywords and link building. One way to over-optimize is to add your keyword to a site too many times!

Site Speed

Google is really paying attention to how quickly your site loads. As of this writing (September 2012) this link was a great tool to check whether your site loads quickly or not, and how you can change it. (https://developers.google.com/speed/pagespeed/insights)

The goal is to have your site to get a speed score of over 90 of 100. They give good suggestions about specific things you can do on your site to increase load speed.

Onsite Linking

You want to include your best keywords in your links to other pages. Even on your site, when you point to your other pages on the site, it helps show what those pages are about. And if you can get links from other people, it is ideal if they also include those keywords, but in a natural way.

SEO Plan 4: User Generated Content

User-generated content is what your audience adds to your site, or what you add to your site as a result of discussions with that audience. These could be in the form of:

- customer testimonials
- product reviews
- discussion boards
- customer driven wikis

Or it could be social sharing such as linking your content to their blog posts, Twitter, Facebook, or Google+ pages.

When you have your audience engaging with you in this manner, it helps you in several ways:

- They are more engaged with you and are getting to know you—so they are more likely to buy.
- They are showing their support or interest in you to their friends—providing you and your products and services with social proof.
- They are showing google that they are engaged with your site—helping your page rank.

When you take the time to do this you are engaging your core niche market and at the same time receiving positive marks in regards to how Google rates you. Google recognizes and takes into consideration this interaction.

Some easy ways to encourage users to contribute is to put Like, Tweet, LinkedIn buttons on your site that make it easy for someone to just click a button and post something about one of your articles or videos.

Good is No Longer Enough

When users give you content, use it wisely. When you get a great customer testimonial or review, or even get mentioned in a video or blog, promote it to your advantage. Find ways to stand out from the crowd. There are so many sites out there; being good is not enough anymore to stand out and remain competitive. You have to really be unique and engaging in what your community really wants. The content has to be information they cannot get anywhere else. You have to create an emotional connection. You have to offer something your customers want.

I know I'm talking a lot about niching down, focusing on targeted keywords and really providing customized content. That's because most of my customers really focus on a small niche. I am not saying that you cannot go for a broad keyword like "leadership," but if you were to go for a keyword like "leadership," you would have to have a really large site that either encompasses everything that people might want to know about leadership, or contains a lot of really good information and be linked out to other sites, so that people know they could come to your site as a valuable resource for leadership. There are not a lot of people who have the budget to do that, so what I recommend often is that people focus on creating a niche community around their content.

SEO Plan 5: Building Your Brand

What is a brand? From Wikipedia: "A brand is thus a product or service whose dimensions differentiate it in some ways from other products or services designed to satisfy the same need."

When we walk into a store, we get a sense of their brand by everything from the lighting and decor to the way the salespeople interact with us. We use that information to decide if we are going to trust that store and buy from them.

Online, our brand is built by our design, which we've covered above, and by people talking about us: linking to us, and typing our name into the search engines.

One goal in building your brand is to increase trust. If you have a brand that people do not know about, then people are not going to trust you and therefore are not going to buy your product or service.

If you are a leadership training academy in Houston and you have no testimonials and nothing on your site that indicates that you really have the chops to do what you say you can do, people are going to be unlikely to buy your services.

Backlinks

I know I covered backlinks earlier in my overview of Panda, and here is more background on the old way of doing backlinks so you really understand the difference.

It used to be that people (including myself) got a lot of backlinks by hiring people to write articles and submitting them to article directories like Ezinearticles, Squidoo, or HubPages. All those sites took a real hit in the Panda update because the content for the most part was not really good.

Since Panda some of those articles still rank highly. Some of them actually harm the sites they link to.

So what kinds of links work now?

Put content on your site that is really newsworthy, noteworthy, interesting, engaging, or educational. These resources are referred to as 'link bait'. They can be case studies, how-to-guides, product tutorials, white papers, or webinars. I know this one site that is very successful. It is for a gardening group and it contains a product tutorial on how to create a self-watering planter. This is great as it brings people to their site where they can be a valuable resource for information and also sell them gardening products.

Other things you want to have on your site to increase trust and build your brand are logos such as TrustE or Better Business logos. Demonstrating that you belong or have been approved by some trusted agency is important in further establishing trust. Stating your privacy policy is another important feature to include on your site as well.

Who is doing this really well? Here are a couple examples. Zappos collects videos from their members praising their products and company. Chick-fil-A does nationwide contests that result in thousands of people mentioning their name, and what you really want is people to mention your name. If you are the Smith Leadership Academy for Non-profits in Houston, you want that name—the Smith Leadership Academy— to be out there. You want people to be noticing it.

Social Media

I would also suggest getting out and promoting yourself and your brand using the various social media formats. Set up a Facebook fan page or a Twitter account. Research indicates that people under 35 do not even really search any more. What they do is ask their friends: they ask their Facebook friends, or their Google+ friends, or they send out a Tweet saying, "So, which leadership training class should we look at?" They find information in new and different ways.

It is crucial for you to be where the fish are. If you are throwing your line into that same pond that you have been throwing your line into all this time and the fish are no longer there, move. If all the fish have moved over to a different pond, you have got to get up and go to that pond. And right now, for a lot of people, that new pond is social media. And I admit, I am slow at getting there too, but it is becoming more and more important. But the faster you learn and adapt, the quicker you are going to benefit and make money. So, get out now and promote yourself and get engaged with social media—Facebook, LinkedIn, press releases, other sites that will bring quality links back to your site.

Chapter Seven—Rebuilding and Preparing for the Future

The first step is to check whether you've been hit by the Panda filter or not.

If your site experienced a dramatic drop in traffic or rankings around the following dates, then probably it was Panda or Penguin.

- Panda Update 1.0 February 24, 2011
- Panda Update 2.0 April 11, 2011
- Panda Update 2.1 May 10, 2011
- Panda Update 2.2 June 16, 2011
- Panda Update 2.3 July 23, 2011
- Panda Update 2.4 August 12, 2011
- Panda Update 2.5 September 28, 2011
- Panda Update 3.0 October 19, 2011

- Panda Update 3.1 November 18, 2011
- Panda Update 3.2 January 18, 2012
- Panda Update 3.2 January 18, 2012
- Panda Update 3.3 February 27, 2012
- Panda Update 3.4 March 23, 2012
- Panda Update 3.5 April 19, 2012
- Penguin April 24, 2012
- Panda Update 3.6 April 27, 2012
- Penguin Update 1.2 May 25, 2012
- Panda Update 3.7 June 8, 2012
- Panda Update 3.8 June 25, 2012
- Panda Update 3.9 July 24, 2012
- Panda Update 3.9.1 August 2012

For example, let's say your rankings for a certain keyword suddenly dropped on July 24. Then the reason for that drop might have been Panda or Penguin. You may also be impacted by one update and not another. Google is constantly tweaking this algorithm to make it more accurate.

Two things you can do if you have been affected by the update. One is to make the changes discussed in this book. The second one is to complain to Google directly. There are a number of places online where you can go and give Google feedback about your site.

What to Do if You've been Hit by Google Panda or Penguin

So you have been hit by Panda or Penguin. After reading this book you have a much better understanding of Panda and Penguin's goals.

It is critical to remember what Google is trying to accomplish, because the next Panda update may affect things in different ways. This book was written in September 2012, and maybe the October update will do things differently; but if you remember the goal, then you will be making the right changes to your site. The changes that I have outlined are the kinds of things that fit in with the long term goals of Google.

So how do you recover? First, make the suggested changes. Take a really good look at your site. Check your Google Analytics, or whatever analytics tool you use to understand what your traffic is doing right now. Take a snapshot, a baseline, so that you can see what your current situation is.

Look at:

- **Keywords:** What keywords are still doing fine, what keywords have been hit
- **Pages:** What pages are doing fine, what pages have been hit
- **Bounce rates:** What are your bounce rates? Are they over 40%? If not, consider whether your keywords are in alignment with your pages
- **Content:** Are people staying on your pages over 2 minutes? If not, consider whether your content is engaging, and if you have enough of it! Is your content fresh?
- **Social media:** Do you have social media buttons on your site? Are they easy to use? If not—add them!

Start by looking at your highest impact pages. What are your money pages? What are the pages that get people to take action? Those are the pages that you want to fix first. You want to protect the pages that are driving a lot of traffic, or if there were pages that were driving a lot of traffic and they got hit, work on those first.

The second thing you want to do is focus on the low hanging fruit.

Broken links: Redesigning your site altogether might take a while, but going through and getting rid of broken links, bad content, and outdated content is fairly quick, generally speaking.

Canonical tags: Changing canonical tags to a single tag usage - you can do it or your webmaster can do it.

Some of these things are going to be pretty quick and some of them are going to take more time. Think about which things you can do that are going to have the highest impact in the least amount of time. One thing that I really suggest people start with is to really think about your keywords, because if you are going too broad in your keywords or going too narrow in your keywords, it is not going to serve you.

If you're a business owner, look for a search engine consultant who understands these concepts. Now that you have read this book, you will have a sense of the questions to ask. You can ask questions about what they will do, ask them where they'll get links for you. If they tell you, "We work with link exchanges," then ask more questions. It is surprising how many SEO consultants are very out of date. If they tell you, "We really need to increase your customer engagement," then they might be somebody who can help you.

One of the things that you are going to want to do or hire somebody to do is A/B testing on your site to find out what changes are working best.

Once all the changes have been made, go back to your Google Analytics, or whatever tool you use, and check your metrics against the baseline.

You want your site visits to go up, your bounce rates to go down, your social media referrals to increase, and your site to load more quickly. Keep in mind though that that the Google Panda update is run every 30 to 40 days. It is a huge program, so it is run periodically. So, even if you get everything going great, you will not see the effects until the next update, and it might take time to get back up in the rankings for those keywords.

Now, if you feel like you have just been penalized wrongly and everything you are doing is good, you can submit a reconsideration request through the Google Webmaster Tools (http://support.google.com/webmasters/bin/answer.py?hl=en&answer=35843)

If your site was knocked down manually—if a human being looked at your site and gave you a low quality score and that is why it dropped in the rankings—then they will reconsider it. If it was knocked down through the Panda filter, or through an algorithmic filter, then you are pretty much just going to have to update the site and wait. But when you submit a reconsideration request, just submit it once.

Other Things to Check (The Tools Section)

You may not have been hit by Panda or Penguin—not yet... But here are some tools that will help you assess your site and determine what changes you should make to help make sure you don't get hit in the future.

As of September 2012 the following sites were free and useful for the following purposes:

Backlink Anchor Text: This is checking that your anchor text is not all using the same words—thus looking like "unnatural" links. (http://www.opensiteexplorer.org/)

Put in your URL and click on the Anchor Text tab to see what anchor text sites are using to link to your site.

You can also use majestic seo (http://www.majesticseo.com/) and review the Top Backlinks tab to get a sense of your anchor text.

If your backlinks are all using basically the same anchor text, then you have two choices to avoid possible impact by Penguin:

1. Get the backlinks removed (Which really is difficult to accept as often people have paid to get these links!)
2. Dilute them with lots of new high-quality links with more 'natural' anchor text.

Speed: You can check your site speed using this tool: https://developers.google.com/speed/pagespeed/insights It also gives you helpful ideas as to how to increase your site speed.

In conclusion, I really hope that you found this book valuable. The most important thing I can tell you at this point is: DON'T WAIT.

Don't wait for your business to get hit. Don't wait and lose traffic, business, and money. Take action on these items today.

As always, if you see anything that you strongly disagree with, especially you search engine people, please send me an email (angelicopub@gmail.com). I'm also happy to answer questions, although I am not taking on any new clients at this point.

This is the latest information that I have from my experience, from reading, and from talking to my associates, who specialize in this field. Thank you very much for reading this book! I hope you check out our other books. I really appreciate you giving us a review of this book. Just click on this link to review the book.

www.ingramcontent.com/pod-product-compliance
Lightning Source LLC
Chambersburg PA
CBHW071033050326
40689CB00014B/3635